WANDERING SUBJECT

For Pandelis & Julia,

"history has given us no chance"

yours,

ELIOT CARDINAUX

Eliot Cardinaux

THE BODILY PRESS
Amherst, MA

Wandering Subject

Copyright © 2025 Eliot Cardinaux

All rights reserved. Except for brief passages quoted for usage in online or print sources (e.g. newspaper, magazine, podcast), no part of this book may be reproduced in any form or by any means, electronic or mechanical, including photocopying and recording, or by any information storage and retrieval system, without permission in writing from the publisher.

This book is set in Cardo and Garamond Premier Pro.
Book design and layout by Eliot Cardinaux.
eliotcardinaux.com

Cover image:
Peter Knapp, *Forest For The Trees*, 2021,
Woodcut, 9 x 13" (22.9 x 33 cm).
All Rights Reserved.
Copyright © 2021 Peter Knapp
PeterKnappArt.com

Bodily Press logo designed by Katya Popova.
popova.space

THE BODILY PRESS
www.bodilypress.com
@thebodilypress

WANDERING SUBJECT

Also by Eliot Cardinaux

Poetry & Chapbooks

On the Long Blue Night
Quiet Labor
Toy Elegy
This Music From Another Room
Island
Rope of Sand
The Ocean from Here to Here
Blue Flowers for Michael Palmer
Starlings

Music

No Dreams Here
Gestures: Schaatsen (with Flin van Hemmen)
American Thicket (with Mat Maneri, Flin van Hemmen,
   & Thomas Morgan)
Sweet Beyond Witness
Odysseus Alone (with Kresten Osgood & Thomas Morgan)
Take Me by the Hand of Darkness (with Will McEvoy
   & Max Goldman)
A Living Past (with Jonas Engel, Asger Thomsen,
   & Simon Forchhammer)
What the Wildflower Witnessed (with Our Hearts as Thieves)
Pavane (with Gary Fieldman)
Out of Our Systems (with Will McEvoy & Max Goldman)
Pain is a Form of Violence Prone to Happiness
   (with Our Hearts as Thieves)
Imminence (with Gary Fieldman)
The Rock Beneath the Tree (with Bram Kincheloe)

in memory of Tristan Honsinger

Table of Contents

BLACK SWANS

I. / 15
II. / 17
III. / 19
IV. / 20
V. / 22
VI. / 24
VII. / 26
VIII. / 28
IX. / 30
X. / 32

ᚠ

BLUE FLOWERS for MICHAEL PALMER

Hyacinth / 39
From the Surface of Time's Ambivalence / 40
Further Blue Flowers / 41
Sometimes / 42
Love / 43
Le Mystère / 44
Favors / 45
Paulownias / 47

Black Swan Song / 48
Absent of Genus / 49
Newport Rebels / 50
Sister / 51
Wisteria / 52
Interest / 53
Forbid / 54
Morning Glory / 55
Indiscriminate Embrace / 56
Alphabetic Postscript / 57
Pure Eyes in the Garden, or *Penthouse* / 58
Inveterate Share of Poppies / 59
A Static Broadcast / 60

YOUR SONG CAST OUT ON THE WILDERNESS

Mile Twenty-Four / 65
Mile Twenty-Five / 66
Mile Twenty-Six / 67
Mile Twenty-Seven / 68
Mile Twenty-Eight / 69
Mile Twenty-Nine / 70
Mile Thirty / 71
Mile Thirty-One / 72
Mile Thirty-Two / 73
Mile Thirty-Three / 74
Mile Thirty-Four / 75
Mile Thirty-Five / 76

Mile Thirty-Six / 77
Mile Thirty-Seven / 78
Mile Thirty-Eight / 79
Mile Thirty-Nine / 80
Mile Forty / 81
Mile Forty-One / 82
Mile Forty-Two / 83
Mile Forty-Three / 84
Mile Forty-Four / 85
Mile Forty-Five / 86
Mile Forty-Six / 87
Mile Forty-Seven / 88

♃

Acknowledgments / 91

Notes / 93

About the Author / 99

☙

You are the keeper of one secret thought
the rose and its thorn no longer stand for

You would like to live somewhere

but this is not permitted
You may not even think of it

lest the thinking appear as words

        Michael Palmer, *First Figure*

BLACK SWANS

*I'm for spare parts,
broken up*

Thom Yorke, *The Eraser*

at last history has given us a chance

Bei Dao, *Sidetracks*

I.

history has given us no chance
two-story ghostly puppets bend
in the wind of protest changing nothing
our sense of hope grown crueler
the repeating autumn
sleepwalking along time's edge
weeping nostalgic cadences

I skip my public speaking class
to learn Ruby, My Dear
behind the stage curtain
as two planes hit the towers
smoke rises on T.V.
smoke rises in the cafeteria
I write the obligatory
letter to my future
self

in a basement venue
in Cincinnati *Kid A*
plays over loudspeakers
history has given us no chance

an Amsterdam drunk plummets
into the canal his face or someone else's
three weeks later on a missing sign
taped to the lamppost outside of *de Fles*
Camus' *The Fall* carried
so much darkness & weight
the next summer the three of us
dancing outside the church & into grief
the three bells
a *little black book* on the floor
of a half-painted Copenhagen apartment

II.

Coming on the Hudson
a skeleton song to cling to
out of exile   & heartbreak
the poem a mess of broken fenders
useless cops & drink tickets

a chestnut in my pocket withers
a gift of not-yet-known
abandonment in spite of new life
on both sides of the ocean

Hawaiian mushrooms
pink & blue paint smears the wall
of a single bedroom in a family house
in Holland   we wake them
fleeing on our bikes
to the *Conservatorium*

in the Gamelan room
waking from deep sleep
on the balcony your face
yellow with paint a hopeless grin
glancing down at my trembling
skeletal thin spectral body
getting up from the piano

I love New York in June, *chèrie*,
how about you? Lee Konitz
three feet away from me at Radio
Perfecto rising in the blood & the sense of
a future   pounding in my veins
these walls grown
thin with the *dust of the private*
litter of the public in transient
safety toward another departure

Hail Mary into unforced
exile out of boredom
exile out of precarity
exile out of love
grey with the balance
of dangerous eyes

III.

one bottle of whiskey
one last meeting
the three of us sudden at Jones Beach
in the back of the car
a flooding toilet
late for the gig again
appearing midway through
no one cares about your dreams
unless you dreamt about them
resting your foot on the bass drum
in Portland Philadelphia D.C.
two packets of rice crackers
one salted   one unsalted
raw   cauliflower

buying a mess of old kitchen
utensils in Boston   that particular set
of salad servers   preparing the piano
in Burlington   detours in the woods
buying weed & reluctantly smoking it
smitten with illusion & fear
rocking back & forth on a stool
at the Outpost the rhythm like raindrops
popping out of expectation

IV.

history gave us no chance
flying down highways in New York
Pennsylvania Ohio Kentucky
Tennessee   the day of the devil's return
June 6th 2006 all shops boarded up
in Johnson City   three devils at the center
of a donut a pickup truck made

hauling stones on a golf cart
through the woods
to make statues
outside of your teepee
history gave us no chance
singing *on the road again*
over & over & over
in the back of the car
& the small dog Ellen
sick from the trash on the floor

my homeland sprawls like a muse
over sunset Bohemia
dirty sheets on a futon
in Crown Heights Brooklyn

an old upright
stands on its haunches
I fall back on the couch
learning to let
the irregular raindrops fall

V.

pocket trumpet in JP
pocket trumpet in the Catskills
no longer caring   resisting
in more & less problematic
ways   my profession
refusing to play
the changes

White Horse whiskey
the flooded apartment
in Washington Heights
you told me to keep my eyes open
in the neighborhood   bullet holes
in the living room window
youth stopping to tie their shoes
you told me to watch my back
history has given us no chance

you danced on stage
at the Bowery Poetry Club   Manhattan
School of Music cafeteria   a spoken
word   not part of the band   banned
from the building   the bow
yanked from under your fingers
a *giant mutant bug*

o multiplicitous *you*
where are our names
what name for the Nazi bunker
I misguidedly equated with your heart
beached in Grenen   in Skagen
beached in the mind's longing
exaggeration
what name for one lesson
we had left to learn
history has given us no chance

VI.

you danced around me in a wolf suit
beating a bass drum   at the center of everything
a trickster invitation to difference   lesson
learned in the folds of an outcast   queerness
divergence   you picked on me   out of
care   gave me all the solos   paid me
I followed your conduction   less
reluctantly then   on fender rhodes
yelling in rehearsal   *wake up*

three hundred dollars in an envelope
outside of Zebulon   I needed it
more desperately than luck
would allow   & yet somehow
it did   under the BQE we watched
Rosemary's Baby   I abstained
in the wake of two wolves
howling over the city
foundation & fratricide

exiled out toward remote isolation
I heard tell of rehearsal & banter
flubbed notes   I sided against those
arrangements   neo-soul winking out
at the end of our era of brazen

& unabashed   electral love   a baritone
intoning   Oedipal irony   clawing
his eyes out absurdly   causing
a tickle in the eyes of your funerary
shock of heads

born in a gulag   he read your biography
out loud   I have it in my inbox   still
I wanted to read your last wishes
fry me up in a skillet   survivor's
breakfast   but I had to drive home
to the hospital   touching the box
a pavane I carried through transition
history has given us no chance

VII.

the stoned lyric of birdsong
red mattress   a railroad apartment
the scuttle of cockroaches   lightswitch
pile-up of dishes   frozen tuna
joint after joint   a medieval melody
played through a Marshall stack
the size of Brooklyn

the eagle never lost so much time
as when he submitted to learn
of the crow   dancing under
the lindens   *under my um-ber-ella*
under the gaze of my paranoia
a man on the roof   my stolen laptop
& it rained all night & then all day
escaping into duo   trombone & alto
over the East River   & under
the Manhattan Bridge

a work of clear genius
recorded over   on Minidisc
a phantom of loops with no lyrics
sticky notes all over the kitchen
wall   *every time he commits a murder*
he puffs his chest out for a medal

things worth repeating in public
in private   at funerals   *making
love over the cake*   complaining
over the deceased   that
reason is a cheap whore

you are crazy for your health
you are crazy for the cane
you walk with   & all this
to say   that you are not crazy
at all   each swan is a picture
a flash   a fragment   a fractured
memory   cluster of what
we are hip to in this world
history has given us no chance

VIII.

hands speak the language of
emotion   which is why we could never
communicate   the word *barrier*
stiff in my mouth like plywood   mouth full
of doritos   back in my native land

hands speak the language of diversion
from a poem of grief   a sleight
of hand   of shyness & all
equivalents   hands speak the language
of uncles   who wanted for the landscape
not to be filled with birches
grown fast for their fuel
right wing   problematic uncles
interviewed onscreen
at Charlottenborg
recalled on the Kombardo ferry

hands speak the language of choirs
singing in Bulgarian   of ravens
that flock toward the unknown
distance of exile
distance of belonging
distance of form
history has given us no chance
in the distance   from here to here

an ocean   blank space on the canvas
the page   blank space where you left me
stranded   in imperative   struggle
in urgency   a toxin   to get
out of our systems   of disability
& law   of prisons & politicians
poets locked up   & dying
young in Aarhus   in Palestine
Hawaii   all problems
in the foundation's eyes

a crack in the wall
a violet that grows there
a missive   a dispatch
Nadezhda Nadezhda
where went the hope
on each side of your name

IX.

how to score was to take
from the black community   how
could it go unpunished   how
could it not   you sent me
a journal entry   as always
scrawled on cheap wide-ruled
paper   torn off at the edges
your vulnerable scrawl
& those lyrics from Amsterdam
a *little black book*   & all the way back
to New York   where
history gave us no chance

transcribing Bessie's Blues
the most unassuming
pieces   fired you up   the trajectory
of Coltrane's life & his home
a few blocks away   in Philly
I will carry your mission
home   to Copenhagen
Providence   Northampton
Maine

how to score new agency
for those who could not see
as well   on bass   on alto
those struggling on piano
to be heard   at Tribes

reading "Rome"   in Williamsburg
new meetings & introductions   long-
lasting   co-conspiracies   in Hudson
The West Village   & Framingham
the portrait of Joseph
where is the father in all of this
a hideous ring   & *what's become*
of baby   history has given us no chance

X.

history gave us no chance
at Crown Fried Chicken   chicken
patties at the best & only bakery
on St. John's Place the lack of trees
& police towers glaring
over our stoop

holding my place in line
at the deli you said   *you look like
Kevin Garnett*   & explained
the forced entry   burglar
shot out the window years before
by an aunt   *words are a sawed-off shotgun*
history has given us no chance

1

BLUE FLOWERS for MICHAEL PALMER

*One should never be completely cured
of one's passion.*

> Marguerite Duras,
> *The Ravishing of Lol Stein*

*And it's inside myself that I must create
someone who will understand.*

> Clarice Lispector,
> *The Passion According to G.H.*

*The one who carries off the obvious on their shoulders
Remembers waves in the salt warehouses.*

René Char, *The Hammer Without a Master*

Hyacinth

for Mette Moestrup

I have not yet stumbled
on blue flowers

& been aware.
But if I sought them out?

In my mother's garden
(who lives in the house

& has not yet planted them
under her mother's tree

to the right of the garden
(whose brother has no tree,

whose father has
no tree, whose tree is

languishing in the shade of
a larger birch), or her father's

tree, to the left of the garden,
which is doing quite well),

I have not yet stumbled on
blue flowers & been aware.

From the Surface of Time's Ambivalence

A broadcast of our non-existence, which terrifies others, comes through the *Radio of Wet Clay* & writes itself in my notebook. About the future distinguished — not by its undecidedly analog or digital construction — but from this present, living future (no, not precisely *living*; the word would be *adjective*) — it is said, that it *risks going forward without an eternity of waiting for this long moment, flowers growing inward, ears of wheat listening to the sun for a sign of salt in the waves beneath the warehouse, blue flowers sensitized to the body, spinning webs of air throughout the body of text*. This neither false nor abrasive certainty of invasion from without by an entity at war with vengeance and familiar with its double, titled *Personality*, lodges itself between signs that announce themselves with wisdom and veneration to the absent attendant in the tower from which the now indecipherable broadcast emanates. The letters scrape themselves against the sand.

Further Blue Flowers

Something's wrong in the music
that's hidden, the film titled

forget me not or *The Compound Wound*
plays over the radio like a song

that is not in fact a film, about
lost enthusiasm. Of the body

& the soul, so much can be said
that is not said, so much can never

be said that is said, like *éxcusez moi*
or *what's on the docket tonight*

The sound before the broadcast
is not music, the broadcast is

not news but a *hang on for dear
life* or *Madonna santisimo*

I swear it is not music
that I play

Sometimes

When there are no words
they are spoken

over the radio, like *chipper*
and *The Urgency of it All*.

The tower falls. The waves
under the warehouse

dry out & leave phantom
movement in the legs

of the attendant
administering the broadcast.

The broadcast, having fallen silent
in the ears of wheat outside

the subterranean window,
registers as *Comfortable*

Conclusion or *what if we never
make it?* Where we are going

depends on who we are
& the *we* is terrible.

Love

Without you the last
5 months would be

madness without company
or *the unreckoning of my*

predicament. In all
your feathers, scales, & fur

I found *these objects unnamed*.
They are many. Some

cannot be lifted up
without *a translucence*

of blue flowers playing
over the radio. The sun

is *not up yet* or *setting
the alarm for 10:00*

Le Mystère

The surface of the town is
how nice or *how nice* is *it?*

When choirs stand up in the midst
of a purple, yawning afternoon

the heart stops black in its past
& whispers *this* is *nice isn't it?* or

what was that back there? Do I dare
remain here? Something about a song

that is sung occasionally, like a
basketweaver's song or a *marriage dance*

hurts even more to the sad, lonely
absent creature at the heart of all

conversation. *Havn* is port,
haven the garden, & ice is *is*.

Favors

Grown from youth's blood,
the little gems or bells

ringing at odd intervals
throughout the morning

or *in the company of
strangers*, at a heightened

pitch. To tell secrets
to the one who will carry

no future for you, is
to *dine indoors* or

*perform an anxiety attack
at the register, smiling.*

But in these trees …
The trees! They are tinged

with red & hang like
warm snow over the street.

No bells. No *dazzling
song* to dance to.

& the *poor man's
flower*, substitute

for coffee, death-quiet
blue at the end of August …

Paulownias

No, I have never seen them.
The road is nameless.

River & stone are nameless,
your voice's absence

speaking its own name.
Like *Butterflies on the Ceiling*

or *the clock stopped at quarter
to ten*. To block out all sound

from below, the everyday
greyness exudes *a warm feeling*, or

the convalescence of church bells.
A willow outside the bank

reaches through tear ducts
to the edge of the frame

Black Swan Song

Why blue flowers?
The word *FOXY*

scrawled in hallucination
across the lawn. To be

sacrificed. Critique
of the code. To enact it.

Victim & aggressor, at least
in language. Appear, naked,

without a temple. More so.
To sacrifice the code.

Absent of Genus

A compersion of blue flowers
titled *All of Us* or *Discipline*

of the Disabled. Unsayable
tumult in the speaking of

names. The unexplained
course this music takes through

The Valley of Uncharted Waters.
That the *Flooded Plateau* aspires

to reach at its diurnal apex.
What grows there, no one

can see, like city rains. Awaited
lovers separate into number

Surfaces grow old
at *The Gate of Registry*.

Newport Rebels

Refusing resolution, the same
blue flowers' translucence

dissolving in catch & conundrum,
a shrine to weather, gutshot

with grief. Gunshot. War.
Grief. Gunshot. War. Enigma.

Grief. Time, too, on its halted way.
Too nice. A tune on ice. Small feat.

Featuring the blast & catastrophe of
something very rough with ragged edges.

Sister

Does the ghost give?
Blue flowers, not quite

white, white-blue, do you
give way? Translucent

blue, I owe you something.
What lives there? I owe you

mercy, & cannot deliver.
Minuscule, giant creature,

which frame are you? This
moon of rice on half a plate.

What lives in the fold decays.
With the aid of what defacement

Wisteria

Death we run toward.
Death we flirt with. Love,

in its alabaster vase
a soap stone chess set.

Laughter's indication
An Atrocity of Surfaces.

Objects linked by dead
verbs. Vindication,

only ever personal.
Lies woven around

a trellis. A suburban,
ritual setting. Artificial

paradise intact, though
the knock on the door

disrupts it. One must
go around & answer.

Interest

To evoke oneself into a play,
the stage, *an absence of petals*

the lighting, *an illness of blue roses.*
The cunt a blue rose. A public, pubic

space, eyed by the rustle of traffic.
A storm of laundry hanging.

A single piano note. To play
oneself into an invocation. Law

as an *interdit*. The door blows
open. The whispers crawl out

Forbid

What happened to the phantom
architecture of a landscape ascribed

as its meaning, *deathly coincidence?* To look
the lifted veil in the face. A moralistic feeling

in the sense of air. Where the salvia bend
purple. Bridge between blue & red. Bees

that hover there. A chance migration
glimpsed through *a possible periphery.*

Gone with the call of the lovers,
a chorus lighting up the day.

Morning Glory

To be lost in one's own milieu
without natural metaphor

or *happy to be here*. Sewn by a
thread in the light of an evening

entirely up to you or into *The Spine
of Night's Mischief, Punished*

Accordingly, the archipelago which,
up until now, has held you, breaks

into air around the neck of a slender
instrument, the song *Pure Eyes*

in the Garden. The music shakes
its little trumpets up the fence.

Indiscriminate Embrace

Little did they know. *In a helix
of parallel madness*, I went

walking. To lie in impossible
fields. The world around me

basked in its silent beauty,
shined in performative

elegance. A puff of aster
glimpsed along an evening

fence. In lieu of my beauty,
beauty made a swarm.

Alphabetic Postscript

The radio has entered
the world. The world

no longer beckons.
It broadcasts. An-

tennae of wheat
stand tall to guard *in-*

defatigable contrast.
Scenes move outside

the silo's halo. They are
not men, working here.

Pure Eyes in the Garden, or *Penthouse*

Lies. Lies bound up in a single world. Two worlds bound up in a single lie. A single lie bound up. In one of two worlds. With a third and fourth world, not bound up with this one. A single non-world, bound up with this, small world. Cruel world, cruel hope. A single hope bound up with this slender cruelty. A single cruelty, made two. In any of these worlds.

Inveterate Share of Poppies

A circumstantial, temporary
privilege. Identities embedded

in the air. A cigarette, a blank
encounter, meeting point between

descriptions, hinge upon which
the door of likeness swings. The road

from *Media of Human Expression*
to *outside the scene you're in*

curves tightly around *The Empty City*.
To push you up against the wall

of a dream, where a little dog yelps
(or was it the woman walking her?)

To satisfy *the incursion of absolute
stillness*, we must in fact be here.

A Static Broadcast

To form an opinion
around the heart,

God of All Stasis,
to have one's existence

removed, *Oblique
Sister*, to negotiate

*The Obstacle of
Something Gone*

Terribly Wrong;
in the *Shattered*

Garden grow these
ever-bluer bells

YOUR SONG CAST OUT ON THE WILDERNESS

tiny house you carry like a violin where the song of springs is –

where to live and, up close to the window grille, calligraph the light of words –

Mireille Gansel,
"soul tongue"

Mile Twenty-Four

What I give to myself & the world
I do to myself & the world.

The poems jeer. A nude
passes through the mirror

& into me. I cry
with my voice outstretched.

& always the same
amorphous question,

loud as I am. What
defense is it not to ask?

Still, I refuse. I come
to you on my knees.

To resist the ellipsis snapped off
at the final word.

Mile Twenty-Five

You do not need
the light that I disclose.

Aestheticize the dark
from which I spring.

Pour from a ceramic
jug the ritual necessity

inherited. Do not disturb
the stillness of the waters.

Long has the road
disappeared. You wake.

The sun comes up
on where you tread.

Destruction follows.
Sawing logs to build

the house of sleep. At
night, encage the moon

& set the bird alight.
Drink from the ash.

Mile Twenty-Six

Those whose line ended,
I know you are steadfast,

proud that a song escaped.
Justification of the wound,

a child with an amputated
family, smiles in the hospital

hall. But you've got it twisted.
Cross my fingers, cross my

toes, & hope to die. Today
the music in my earbuds

soars, & my heart stays
put. There is land there.

Mile Twenty-Seven

Your voice lodged in a place.
Your gut lodged in its name,

& moving toward a break. A
stormless autumn, quiet, still,

& leaking blood the color of
another's name. The yellow

leaves. The yellow leaves, &
blue sky between them. White

clouds. White clouds & eerie
wind. A bunch of people

walking out in it. A stain-
less autumn in your name.

Mile Twenty-Eight

Oil. Oil without a home.
Tent cities. Encampments

of objects. Very real objects.
Throbbing hearts, & spirits

without bodies. Shrines without
churches or temples. Spirits

annoyed with houses. Spirits
annoyed with themselves, &

laughing. Bodies toyed with.
Others toying with spirits. Churches.

Temples. Flags out front. Bodies ready
to get up, & silence, a broken chord.

Mile Twenty-Nine

If this is moral, this
need, this call to action,

to do better, grass come up
in clumps, the jumping

worm, the new seed scattered,
stone extracted, this madness

then, what is it? A fire
under you, explosive pop

of snare, & scattered cymbal
dancing in new buoyancy,

the clink of glass on glass
& what lies beneath.

Mile Thirty

We act in part to save
ourselves. I cannot

escape my heart. Drive
your tongue through it.

Bees make honey out of
the dead. Fall through

this poem, long
as you wish.

Mile Thirty-One

At night I find you
missing from me.

Somnambulant, I
long for tenderness,

dead friend. Do you
hear your song cast

out on the wilderness? This
summer night on the cusp

of November. Nothing is
still. Even the frogs hear it.

Mile Thirty-Two

Neutral, not-quite neutral,
whom have you left in

the lurch? Whom have you
let go? Who gets to do as

they please, drive off, signs
bristling in the back seat?

What do the signs say? We
will protect you, & only you.

What will you give to us?
Oaths, undone by silence.

Mile Thirty-Three

Pawns. Fall back on
this time. Every which

way. Hither. To & fro.
Lay your blanket of

two dimensions on
my lap. This privilege

to stand between you
& what you are after.

Whom. Pursuit. Pur-
suance. Psalm. & the fruit

of whose endeavor.
Sum in the sky.

Mile Thirty-Four

From now on, no margins.
Just a scribble outside

the page. A downward
leap of the gut, red, blue.

In these states one can only
hope

to be taken as ill, schizo-
phrenic, denatured,

multiple. An alcoholic
gauze over the eye.

A sting to suffer. Toy
with the arm outstretched.

Clothing that smells
of cigarettes

& shower water.
Coke can left behind.

Mile Thirty-Five

Amidst the ongoing,
concern. No care, no

tangible resource
can stop you

moving along at a pace,
your heart transfixed

with the journey
of everything

but grief. What
grievance, what

price to pay?
Can you give?

Can you give
a little?

Mile Thirty-Six

Hard not to feel small.
By bent light I rewind

two stanzas, couplets
mixed & broken up,

reforming in units
of discrete sound

backwards,
discretion, not

the republic's
strong suit.

Sometimes it's
hard to tell, alone

& broke with it,
the work meeting

up with itself more
than we. Surreal

act to be part of
& parcel up.

Mile Thirty-Seven

Wandering subject,
what is the quickest

way to oblivion?
Tenured in the crotch

of your mad disposability,
I wonder all beings

left behind into a
cascading, downward

flight of my own.
A rope of sand

renewing liminal
rescue dissolves

in front of you.
Further ahead,

will you still wonder
yourself what all

the fuss is about,
the elusive safety?

Mile Thirty-Eight

A wounded bird
I stumbled into

what you found.
Elusion made

your heartbreak
daunting, this

crafted loneliness
a soft coercion

into synthesis.
What hurt, now

melody, your
fingers moving,

sound coming out
between depressions,

hands shaking
over the keys.

Mile Thirty-Nine

Tightrope, re-
turn, I move

to take credit
or blame. As one

who steps lightly,
not to disturb

the sleeping,
dance & all

is courage. I
think & I mull,

pursuit, & I
can't just win.

Mile Forty

Time oceanic
& violent, Thursday

clamors for the door.
Who is washing away

the sanctity, complicit,
boundless, & abrupt.

Flooded lawns, brown
fields, & time messianic.

Uncrossed, despite its
betrayals, dampening.

Mile Forty-One

Strange, that your home
is brokenness. How else

would it happen. Of course
the world is as it is. All told,

you are not surprised. Not
torn, you can walk away.

A cigarette bears black
ink to the lungs, wheeze,

song, & whistle. Pause to
think. Bare open the wound.

Mile Forty-Two

Snow day, & as I walk
the ground melts in the air.

No agency, if calculation
keeps the abyss below you, maybe

some small change in the light,
keeps the advantage

absolutely. In this world
we say, *they were part*

*of this world, & they are
missed*. A real thing

also misses
you, & lives.

Mile Forty-Three

Greet me. Always
the world stands still

when all is chaos. I
reiterate the choices,

left, right, left to myself
as I walk into day. To go

into hail & comfort
knowing I must

slow down & not being
able. To twist & turn in

the night & its laden
surround of sound.

Mile Forty-Four

I love you & I'm in
love with you,

essence & action
mooring the unfixed

tropes of meaning,
italic & stalemate

with the world. Our
run-on sentence.

How many years
will we make love

in this cell to pitches,
letters to the dead

& to each other,
U-O-Ye-Vo-Li?

Mile Forty-Five

When Tongo read,
one could pick up

fragments, but mostly
we heard the contested-

ly legible noise of
history. A radio tuned

to every station at once.
Our voices, plural. When

Tasha came up
& said *happy birthday*,

it was hers, & I said
thank you. You too.

But it was not mine.
The store performed

its entitlement,
gift after gift.

Mile Forty-Six

Versed in her-
metic heresy

we dissected
our pronoun.

Mackey's orphan
orphic noise

an estrangement
the burnt book

left behind. Ash &
art made a public

litter of
private spaces'

inexhaustibly
tropic turning,

burn & level's
sixth circle

announcing
a curfew.

Mile Forty-Seven

Our bodies come
to rest. A serene expanse, but

how did I end up here?
Differentiation names us.

All is many, multiple. A
conflagration toward

which I withdraw. I am
disappearing. How far

below, how distant
the Earth is.

फ

Acknowledgments

My sincere thanks to the editors of the following journals in which these poems first appeared:

"Hyacinth" in *Wild Roof Journal.*

"From the Surface of Time's Ambivalence" in *Heavy Feather Review.*

"Absent of Genus" in *Smoke and Mold.*

"Mile Thirty-Seven" in *antiphony.*

"Mile Forty," "Mile Forty-One," and "Mile Forty-Two" in *Lamplit.*

My deepest love and gratitude to my life partner Shana Bulhan, who gave me the title of this collection, who offered invaluable edits and suggestions, and who has been there the whole way through. I cannot overstate the importance of this relationship, poetically, emotionally, and intimately, for me.

My gratitude to Peter Knapp for our ongoing collaboration, and for the generous use of his beautiful woodcut.

Special thanks to Tasha Robbins for her camaraderie, whose "Forget-Me-Nots" earlier graced the cover of my chapbook *Blue Flowers for Michael Palmer* (Bodily Press, 2024).

Big thanks to Ian Fishman, for tugging this boat along.

My thanks, also, to Niamh Timmons for their friendship and ongoing support of my work with The Bodily Press.

Lastly, profound thanks to Andrew Mossin for being a deeply attuned first reader of this work.

Notes

The epigraph at the beginning of this collection is taken from Michael Palmer's poem "Voice and Address," from *First Figure* (North Point Press, 1984), also collected in *Codes Appearing* (New Directions, 2001).

Black Swans

The epigraphs at the beginning of "Black Swans" are taken respectively from Thom Yorke's song "Black Swan" off the album *The Eraser* (XL Recordings, 2006), and from section XII of Bei Dao's *Sidetracks*, Jeffrey Yang, translator (New Directions, 2024).

In section I, "Ruby, My Dear" is a song by Thelonious Monk. *Kid A* is an album by Radiohead (Capital Records, 2000).

In section II, "Coming on the Hudson" is a song by Thelonious Monk. The phrase *"dust of the private / litter of the public"* is taken from Bei Dao's poem "Year's End," collected in *At the Sky's Edge*, David Hinton, translator (New Directions, 2001). "I love New York in June" is the opening lyric from "How About You," a song composed by Burton Lane, with lyrics by Ralph Freed, from the film *Babes on Broadway* (Metro-Goldwyn-Mayer, 1941).

In section III, the phrase *"no one cares about your dreams / unless you dreamt about them"* is derived from the title of a song by saxophonist/composer Pete Robbins off the album *Waits and Measures* (Playscape, 2006).

In section VI, *Rosemary's Baby* refers to the film by Roman Polanski (Paramount Pictures, 1968).

In section VII, the phrase *"the eagle never lost so much time / as when he submitted to learn / of the crow"* is taken from William Blake's "Proverbs of Hell," which can be found in *The Marriage of Heaven and Hell: A Facsimile in Full Color* (Dover, 2012). The phrase *"under my um-ber-ella"* is taken from Rihanna's song "Umbrella" off the album *Good Girl Gone Bad* (EMI Records, 2007). The phrase *"& it rained all night & then all day"* is taken from Thom Yorke's "And It Rained All Night" off *The Eraser*. Loosely referred to in this section, "Fractured Memories" is a solo piano composition by the late trumpeter/composer Daniel Levine, from the author's debut solo piano album *No Dreams Here* (self-released, 2014).

In section VIII, "*Nadezhda Nadezhda*" (Russian, for "Hope") refers to Nadezhda Mandelstam and her memoir *Hope Against Hope* (Random House, 1999), and also to Nadezhda Alliluyeva, Joseph Stalin's second wife, who committed suicide in 1932.

In section IX, "Bessie's Blues" is a song by John Coltrane. The phrase *"what's become of baby"* is the title of a song by The Grateful Dead off the album *Aoxomoxoa* (Warner Brothers/Seven Arts, 1969). Loosely referred to in this section, "The Mission" is an as-yet unrecorded composition (as of the publication of this book) by Daniel Levine.

In section X, the phrase *"words are a sawed-off shotgun"* is a line from the song "Jigsaw Falling Into Place" off the album *In Rainbows* by Radiohead (XL Recordings, 2007).

Blue Flowers for Michael Palmer

The epigraphs at the beginning of "Blue Flowers for Michael Palmer" are taken respectively from Marguerite Duras' novel *The Ravishing of Lol Stein* (Knopf Doubleday, 2013), and Clarice Lispector's novel *The Passion According to G.H.* (New Directions, 2012). The two lines by René Char are from "The Oracle of the Great Orange Tree" ("*L'Oracle du grand oranger*"), originally written in French and collected in *Le Marteau sans maître suivi de Moulin premier* (Éditions Gallimard, 2019), here translated by Eliot Cardinaux.

"Hyacinth" is inspired by the Danish poet Mette Moestrup's poems "Before Noon" and "Afternoon in the Winter Garden" translated by Katrine Øgaard Jensen and published in *Spoon River Poetry Review, Volume 48, Issue 1, Summer, 2023*.

The last line in "Sometimes" is derived from the title of Cameron Awkward Rich's *The Terrible We: Thinking with Trans Maladjustment* (Duke University Press, 2022).

"*Le Mystère*" is titled after the album *Le Mystère des Voix Bulgares* by the Bulgarian State Radio and Television Female Vocal Choir (Disques Cellier, 1975/Nonesuch, 1985).

"Black Swan Song" is titled after Thom Yorke's "Black Swan" from *The Eraser* (XL Recordings, 2006). The song was featured in Richard Linklater's film *A Scanner Darkly* (Warner Independent, 2006) based on the science fiction novel of the same name by Philip K. Dick (Ballantine Books, 1977/Orion Limited, 2006). The poem also nods to Kali Malone's album *The Sacrificial Code* (Ideal Recordings, 2019).

"Newport Rebels" is titled after an album led by Charles Mingus and Max Roach (Candid, 1961). The album was recorded live in 1960 at "an alternative Newport Jazz Festival in protest of Newport's conservative and increasingly commercial booking policy" (Scott Yanow, *AllMusic*. Source: *Wikipedia* entry for "Newport Rebels").

"Interest" nods to Jonathan Glazer's film *The Zone of Interest* (A24, 2023), and alludes to a scene from Alan Benson and Daniel Wiles' documentary, *Marguerite Duras — Worn Out With Desire To Write* (Films Media Group, 1985).

In "Morning Glory," the phrase "Pure Eyes in the Garden" nods to a line in René Char's poem "*Bel Édifice et les pressentiments*" | "Handsome Edifice and Presentiments," also from *Le Marteau sans maître* (Gallimard): "Pure eyes in the woods / Seek in crying a head fit to live in" (translation by the author, published in *Tupelo Quarterly*, July 31st, 2023).

Your Song Cast Out on the Wilderness

This section continues the long-form serial poem begun in "Rope of Sand," collected in *The Ocean from Here to Here* (Bodily Press, 2025).

The epigraph at the beginning of this section is taken from Mireille Gansel's poem "*langue d'âme*" ("soul tongue"), from *Maison d'âme* (La Coopérative, 2018), here translated by Eliot Cardinaux.

"Mile Twenty-Eight" calls up a fragment from Paul Celan's

Microliths They Are, Little Stones (Contra Mundum Press, 2020): "Endnote: Poetry "a shrine with no temple" <cf. Heidegger: Hölderlin>" (translation, Pierre Joris).

"Mile Twenty-Nine" calls up Alejandra Pizarnik's *Extracting the Stone of Madness*, Yvette Siegert, translator (New Directions, 2016).

In "Mile Thirty-Two," the line "Oaths, undone by silence" is derived from Paul Celan's poem "All Souls" | "*Allerseelen*," as translated by Ulrich Baer in *Remnants of Song: Trauma and the Experience of Modernity in Charles Baudelaire and Paul Celan* (Stanford University Press, 2000).

In "Mile Thirty-Six," *By Bent Light* is the title of a chapbook by Nathaniel Mackey (Bodily Press, 2025).

In "Mile Forty-Five," the name "Tongo" refers to the poet Tongo Eisen-Martin. The name "Tasha" refers to the painter Tasha Robbins.

In "Mile Forty-Six," "Mackey's orphan / orphic noise" refers both to "'The Song Sung in a Strange Land': An Interview with Nathaniel Mackey" by Andrew R. Mossin in *Iowa Review: Volume 44, Issue 3, Winter 2014-15*, and to the title of Patrick Pritchett's poetry collection *Orphic Noise* (Dos Madres Press, 2017). Also called up in this poem is Pritchett's essay "How to Write Poetry After Auschwitz: The Burnt Book of Michael Palmer," collected in *Make it Broken: Toward a Poetics of Late Modernism* (Black Square Editions, 2025).

About the Author

ELIOT CARDINAUX is a poet, pianist, composer, publisher, and translator working at the edges of the lyric and improvised music. The author of *On the Long Blue Night* (Dos Madres, 2023), the trio of *Quiet Labor*, *Toy Elegy*, and *This Music From Another Room* (Bodily Press, 2024), and *The Ocean from Here to Here* (Bodily Press, 2025), as well as numerous chapbooks, Eliot has also produced and appeared on over a dozen albums of original music, including *American Thicket* (Loyal Label, 2016), *Out of Our Systems* and *Pavane* (Bodily Press, 2022), and most recently *Imminence* (self-released, 2024) with USAmerican percussionist Gary Fieldman. He holds a bachelor's degree in contemporary improvisation from The New England Conservatory of Music, and an MFA in creative writing, with a focus on poetry, from the University of Massachusetts in Amherst. Eliot's poems and translations have appeared in *Jacket2*, *Meridian*, *Bennington Review*, *Tupelo Quarterly*, *California Quarterly*, *The Arts Fuse*, *Solstice*, *Spoon River Poetry Review*, and elsewhere. At present, he co-leads an American trio with bassist Will McEvoy and drummer Max Goldman, works in a duo with Gary Fieldman, leads his own Danish Quintet, and is a member of the international poetry and free-improvisation ensemble, Our Hearts as Thieves. He performs throughout Europe and the Northeastern United States. He has taught literature and writing at UMass Amherst, and music as a postgraduate mentor at the Copenhagen Rhythmic Music Conservatory in Denmark. He works as a bookseller at Amherst Books, and as founding editor of The Bodily Press.

Author photograph by poet Shana Bulhan • shanabulhan.com

THE BODILY PRESS
bodilypress.bandcamp.com
www.bodilypress.com
@thebodilypress